Violins

of my Soul

Poems of the Heart

Thomas Theophilus

Quantum Discovery

A LITERARY AGENCY

Violins of My Soul
Copyright © 2024 by Thomas Theophilus

Library of Congress Control Number: 2024916459

ISBN
978-1-964982-47-2 (Paperback)
978-1-964982-48-9 (eBook)
978-1-964982-46-5 (Hardcover)

TABLE OF CONTENTS

DID I TOUCH YOU… THERE?

Love was in her eyes as the candle flickered,
A kiss so tender it took her breath;
Passion from her lips as the wax dripped,
And she thought, was it a kiss, a kiss of death?
Passion to her was like a fine painting,
With each touch came moments of desire;
In her eyes showed the need of wanting,
And each kiss set his soul on fire!
O tender heart, how did I touch you… there?

© April 26, 2015

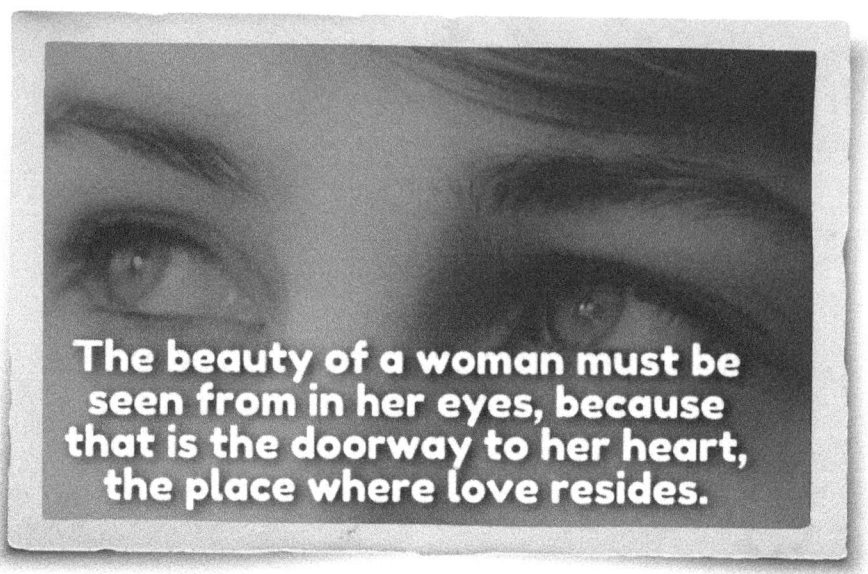

The beauty of a woman must be seen from in her eyes, because that is the doorway to her heart, the place where love resides.

AN ABSOLUTE

Surely she will believe me, I hope!
Surely she knows I love her, I hope!

Surely tomorrow will bring sunshine,
And light the path of her walk, I hope,
But tomorrow is not a guarantee, I know.

So I must tell her today that I love her
And when ask if she is loved, she can say,
"That's an absolute, he told me just today."

© October 16, 2005

BRANDY WITH SLOW SIPS

There are so many lonely hearts,
So many empty souls,
So sad to admit that this is true,
And in life it takes its tolls!

In restaurants I sit and watch people
There is no laughter, they don't talk –
On the cell phones they sit and text,
And some are so fat they can't walk!

Here we are under the canopy of stars,
A speck in the world of time and space –
A broken society – of worry and pain
Where everyone now gets in your face!

Social media has become our downfall,
Where emotions draw thin!
But in all there still lies an inner need
To know the truth from within.

Brandy with slow sips I sit in thought,
Time goes on – it doesn't skip a beat,
Each generation will survive somehow,
But one day our maker we'll all meet.

© November 1, 2019

Never let an old flame burn you twice

FOREVERMORE MY LOVE

The night brought dreams of an old flame,
As we walked in the garden hand in hand –
Whispers of love from a woman to a man
Then in a quiet voice she call out my name –
Yesterday is something we can never blame!
We have to forgive – I know that we can
Regrets serve no purpose – so take a stand –
Love in our hearts – it remains the same!
"I will love you forever!" cried she…
Just let yesterday go – her words of plea –
With tender lips, "Kiss me like no tomorrow,
And know that I will always love thee!"
Forget the past – it only brings you sorrow –
We make mistakes in life – so close the door,
And know! "I will love you forevermore!"

© August 30, 2021

4

O MAGIC WOMAN

Love, desire, run, and don't be late
O magic woman please don't hesitate!
More passion then a heart can hold,
As your mystery is about to unfold:
Thoughts in my mind can't comprise,
This beauty before me dazzles my eyes!
The honey dripping from your mouth,
Makes my blood want to flow south!
O magic woman please don't hesitate!
The night beckons, love is thy fate.
Champagne is chilling in the ice,
The music soft and low just to entice,
A fireplace hisses an ominous sound-
Desire is devious, and passion abound.

© February 3, 2014

PLEASURES IN THE NIGHT

When you play, this is where it's at!
And tonight you'll make the mark
Like the screams of an alley cat
That prowls in the shadows of dark.

The feelings of love you can't hide
Under the sheets of silken sheath
Your sharp nails cling and glide
Like daggers stabbing you to death.

The smooth touches lure you in –
The sweet kisses upon your skin:
Needs that fan your lustful flame –
Are only desires your heart can claim.

The pleasures in the night, you shout!
Suppressed emotions need to come out!
A body out of control then you let it go –
And taste a love that you need to know.

© November 20, 2011

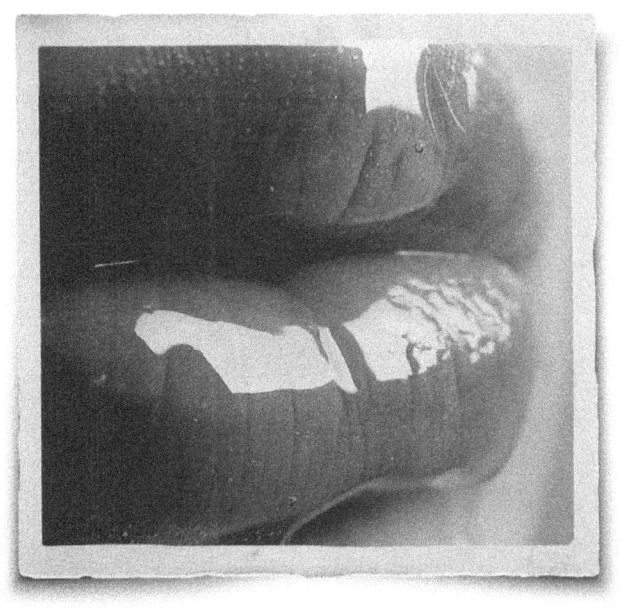

OCTOBER KISS

A kiss, tender as the touch of a child,
It is given like the taste of wine;
Like passion there is no way to gauge,
Lips so hot it blows your mind!
Beads of sweat where desire wants to dine.
Innocence needs to cry – lust in our eyes are fed, -
But cries, only a heart that is in pain,
The sheets are wet – bodies entangled in bed,
An October kiss can never be in vain!
This will surely last forever, we think, -
Drowning in desire – it's of love we drink.

Faces of desire but can one's eyes bear to look
At the fibers of our soul;
Was it love or desire, pages in a romance book –
Tomorrow when we awake – truth we'll know!

© October 17, 2015

7

SONNETS OF PASSION

Passion: O what you do to my soul
You are like shadows of illusion: how you
captured my heart!
And at night: you come quietly as if to say
"I know that love is the panacea that waits
to play its part."

Yes I know you, you come in a moment, and
You surround my sadness of tears that only
passion can do
Why is this! It's like you are hiding from me,
Waiting until my soul cries out for you.

But it's you, my sweet dear passion for love.
You are a tranquility of desire: so enticing
Like a ripened fruit, dangling from a vine –
lips burning
I crave to taste your juice that leaves my mouth
wanting more
The darkness cannot contain you from me -
Your light rushes in from years of yearning.

© March 16, 2015

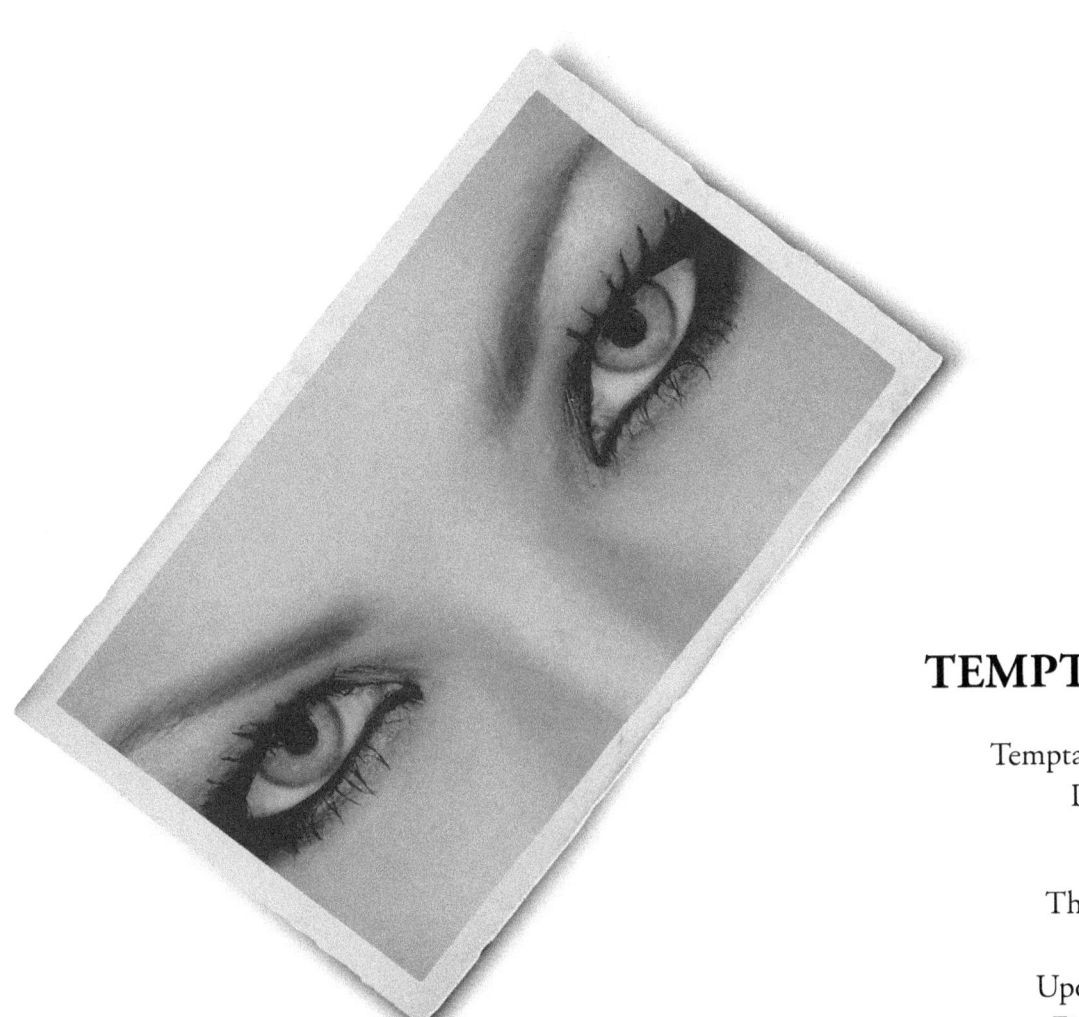

TEMPTATION

Temptation at dawn
Desire starves
For love.

The night longs
For passion
Upon the sheets.
Fingers touches
Sensation lingers
The night taunts
Every emotion;
And she teases
With her eyes

The heart cries
Loves'
Compromise.

Temptation at dawn,
Can love be wrong?
The heart longs
For desire.

She teases
Passion cries aloud;
Burning with desire
Bodies on fire…
Love
It's never proud!

© May 11, 2016

THE KISS

I think it is only fair that you should know…
With prior warning maybe your face won't glow.
When our lips touch your inner soul will be burned!
From all this hot passion you so yearn.
Your blood will flow like a mighty river setting its pace
Like the sweetness of honey… just right for the taste.

There will be chills running up and down your spine
With this single kiss my love we will entwine.
Your erogenous zones have never known such fire
With such a thirst for love you so desire.
Can the heart stand this beating, the gentleness of pain?
Like the rose petals in the pounding rain.

This abstract notion that you had been kissed before
Now these thoughts will leave you forevermore.
Your muscles will expand and places become wet
This I can assure you so please don't fret.
Your veins will thrill like lighting flashing in the sky
Struggle if you may, but you know not why.

The suction from our mouths like a slow gentle rain
So wet and wild, but you won't complain.
Unconditionally, totally free like grapes give into wine
I am yours and you are mine
Feeling new emotions the ones that have never been
Fight my love, but you know I am going to win!

© '1998

UNFORGETTABLE

Life.
It has all come to this.
The thought of you.
Each moment
Filled with yesterday
-is it not true?-
The spirits seeking
images of you,
ever longing,
searching, needing
heart bleeding,
and grieving
over you.
Time passes.
Time stands still.
The dreams-
Madness raving
Before the night finds day,
Restfulness
Before dawn,
As though the world died,
And I'm all alone,
Despair is upon me
Without any care,
You know my heart is sad
But how can you see.
The dreams-
Darkness is an empty plot

As life finds its lot
In time,
Regrets of yesterday,
What "could've been?"
But "what is"
My tears...
It was me!
Not forgotten years
When we become frail.
And time will tell,
Like kisses of morning dew,
When I only thought of you
And my heart was glad
For a love that was true-
I shall cherish each day that
Binds me to you,
And I shall always regret
That you are not here
In stone this is set.
My life
Stored in shadows-
Tormented in my head,
The nights I dread
Filled with sadness
Without you.
Darling,
The times I remember
Makes me sad,
Why did you leave?
Why do I grieve?

If I could see you once more
Then my heart would be glad
Just a tender word,
Your gentle smile
The silence unheard,
Spoken with your eyes
Amidst my loneliness.
I need you!
To fill my day,
To show me the way,
I falter without you
I don't know where to begin,
Where will it end?
I'm at the end of my rope!
Please give me some hope,
Time passes-
-I try to sleep-
Life is bliss,
Longing to taste your lips
The sweetest of your kiss,
When I draw my last breath,
Know that I loved you till my death.

© March 10, 2004

THESE EYES

I have seen the sun rise over the mountains of blue,
And the sunset when the day was through.
The misty fog rising from a gentle summer's rain,
And the tears that weep from a heart in pain.

I have seen the innocence of a child as he plays,
And at bedtime when he knells to pray.
The shaky first steps as he makes his way,
And words he tries to form but can barely say.

I have seen the willows as they sway in the wind,
And I have given thought to you my friend.
I have seen the hurt in a soul that won't mend,
And the sadness that seems to never end.

I have seen the red roses that bloom in springtime,
And I saw the grapes before they were wine.
I saw the lilies standing in the field so proud and fine,
And the blissful effort of an eagle making her climb.

I have seen the mighty ocean crashing its gentle shore,
And the winter winds pounding upon a battered door.
Why am I blinded by the truth and is it just my demise?
Surely you saw the love I hold for you in "these eyes?"

© September '2000

IT'S ONLY ME

The moon beams shone through the window, and reflected from your hair
You were sleeping so peacefully…the wind lightly blew the curtains
Standing and watching you for a long while…finally I enter your dream
I touched your hair and stroked it gently as it falls through my fingers
There was a serene look upon your pretty face…as to say I'm glad you came.
The smell of you reminds me of rose petals after the summer rain
I can feel the warmth of your body penetrating my soul…
Lying down beside you…careful not to wake you…I draw you close
My heart is pounding like ten thousand drums…how can you not hear it?
It's only here that I feel a part of your perfect world.
Like silk on satin my hands trace your smooth thighs and buttocks…
Your breathing gets louder…and then it subsides slowly
With whispers softly I say…I love you more than life itself…
You move slightly as though you heard my words…I think to myself
No one will ever hurt you again…as long as you are in my arms.
If we could only melt into one…if our hearts were welded together
All of our fears would just go away…then the sky would be clear again
If we could hold onto this moment…surely our love can cure all of the pain…
Our troubles of this life would dissipate into yesterday…
Then tomorrow's destiny would be ours.
Now the sun flickers through the tall pines with the dawning of a new day
The time has come for me to go…I rise slowly and stand in the shadows…
Your eyes open, and you just lie there for the longest time…does she know?
You turn towards me and I can see tears well in your eyes…I cry out!
I Love you! But it's all in vain for you can't hear me… I will never leave you!
Whispering through my tears I say…"It's only me."

© Jan '2000

LOVE DONE RIGHT

When I hear your voice,
My heart skips a beat
It has no choice . . .
Like an after dinner treat!
Look at those skinny jeans,
O let me in!
Lust spinning in my head,
And lips I want to kiss –
I'll carry you to my bed . . .
O your warm touch I miss,
Where have you been?
Wrinkled sheets . . .
There is a silent hush
As you lie on your back
Blood in our veins rush –
The music plays low,
The wine is chilling . . .
It's passion we know –
And our hearts are willing,
Taking love to the edge,
Where nothing matters!
Like hanging on a ledge:
Your erogenous zones are
Like reactors . . .
And when I touch places
You will become wet!
We rolled the dice,
And we placed a bet –

The sheets show traces
Love making at its best . . .
Hearing your whispers
"I love you!"
Echoes into the night –
And when we're through
"It was love done right!"
Now we can rest…

© January 20, 2024

REFLECTIONS OF MY TEARS

Why is today any different from any other?
I stare into the mirror as I do every day
Could it be because I see my life, as it ought to be?
The reflection of me that I let no one see.

So many people come to look, but they don't see me
They don't see the person I am and want to be
God made the roses with beauty beyond compare
In time I also will fade then who if any will care?

Do you know I like to sit and listen to the trains?
Smell the sweetness of honeysuckles after the rain
Old folks telling their tales I smile as the stories unfold
Even the silence of a breeze can comfort my soul.

Why do my eyes well up as I am trying to reason?
Is it the reality of what you maybe believing?
This mask that I put on to start each day
If you only knew the real me what would you say?

By the roadside a single rose I stooped to gather
If it had been a thousand my love would it matter?
For I took the time and gave thought of you
All the treasures in my heart if you but only knew.

For hours I can watch the butterflies kiss the daises
Lie on a river bank and just be lazy
The wonder in a child's eyes as it takes its first step
The peaceful dreams of you even as I slept.

If you would take the time to see more than just the exterior
Surely the love in my heart for you is more superior
Will you not take a chance at love, with all of its fears?
Is that love in your eyes or just "Reflections of my tears?"

© July '1999

ALMOND EYES

I feel you from inside-
Your spirit flows in me,
Tingling through my body -

The sudden rush of my heart,
As the tears well in your eyes -
I can see those sexual desires,
From the path you leave behind -

So I just lie here -
Where silent thoughts reside,
Looking into your almond eyes.

© January 30, 2011

DANCE ME TO THE END

The music played in a distant town,
As we poured the whiskey down –
The beauty I held I didn't know:
Her eyes were looking back at me,
We just showed up there, not a date,
But I remember the kisses so great!
A night of two hearts out of control –
And in her eyes of passion I drown:
So now… what shall we do…
Entangled hearts – just us two –
Love or infatuation we had found,
Knowing the night wouldn't be again
As the music played in a distant town:
O dear lover! Dance me to the end…

© August 29, 2020

A LOVE SICK FOOL

I feel you near me
In so many ways,
But how can I remember
Those times of yesterdays,
The games a heart plays,
Of a love sick fool!

I loved you so much
At least it now seems,
The night will linger
Of you in my dreams;
The moon casts beams,
Of a love sick fool!

So I look back at
My heart filled with sorrow!
And sadness I only know –
For there is no tomorrow
And no time I can borrow
For a love sick fool!

© July 22, 2017

26

IT'S NOT MY FAULT

A double standard of facts! I mean all –
You always want things your way, in fact
You ran this train off the track…
I requested a do over – if you can recall?
Then you bring up the past, that was small,
It's a simple discussion, but you have no tact!
When I speak, all you can do is counteract –
I state the truth, but you want to have a brawl,
Emotions are always at play! It's a mind game
I'm not here to make you feel insecure, a heart
Needs understanding, what's with all the blame,
It's not my fault! I was just explaining my part –
We're at an impasse – forgiveness we must seek,
But the trouble is – now I'm afraid to speak!

© December 20, 2017

YOU CAUGHT ME

Over the cliff I go,
My curiosity – I want to know:
What are the secrets that you hold?
You bent over and I took a glance
Guessing what's in those pants?

In a moment you stop and turn,
You caught me – what did I learn?
I'm thinking I need to be cool –
That is the golden rule . . .
After all we have never met,
And there is no reason for you to fret!

But you almost gave me a heart attack,
And my composure I can't get back –
Just thinking of getting you in the sack!

© January 18, 2024

O PASSION! O PASSION!

O Passion! O Passion
Why taunt me so…
You mess with my heart
But I can't let you go!

You over take me
In moments of desire,
And in lonesome times
You burn like a fire!

And O Passion! O Passion!
You play with my head;
Reflection of beauty
That lures me to her bed.

And I wonder why,
But I can only sigh…
Remember you promised,
That you'd never cry!

Well dear passion…
Why taunt me so…
You brought me heartaches,
But I can't let you go!

© May 21, 2018

A BLANK CANVAS

What thing shall I say to you?
Thy colors bleed from your armor.
What thing shall I say to you?
Lighting flashing from the sky
Or violins screaming in my head,
Drawing sounds within my soul
Like a thousand drums pounding
Until my spirit burst free.

What is this pain burning inside!
Like an arrow piercing my heart
How can I resolve this inter need

Before the arrows finds its mark.
How does inspiration grow wings?
In a frozen spirit harden by time.
Shall it be awaken by a new day?
That hides in a darkness of fear.

Thy boundaries are an empty pit
As ideas give in to idol thoughts
But thy vastness engages my soul,
Like the fibers of my last breath.
Then, my eyes open to a renewal
Of a moonlit oceans misty waves,
The crashing sounds are unlocked
And passion flows with little work.

You have taken me out of my despair
And broken my spirit into little pieces,
Thy colors bleed from your armor.
Because of a blank canvas before me,
It now seems you will have your say.
Today thy brushstrokes of brightness
Thy rainbow is like an endless river
And my emptiness is filled once more.

© March 4, 2004

HOOKED ON HUGS

Isn't it wonderful what a hug can do?
It can make you smile when you're feeling blue,
Or it can simply say, "I love you."
A hug is like" Hey I'm glad to see you again,
I've missed you, where have you been?"
A hug can cure the smallest pain,
And bring you rainbows after a rain.

A hug embraces you with its warmth and charms,
Maybe that's why God has given us arms?
We cannot survive in this world without touch,

Our hands reaching out for someone to clutch.
So if you should see a soul that seems to be low,
Give them a big hug and watch their face glow.

Hugs are wonderful for fathers and mothers,
Sweet little sisters and even grumpy brothers.
When our hearts are pressed against each other's,
It's the most wonderful feeling you will ever discover.
Old folks sit on a park bench
holding hands and cuddle,
Even football players hug as they
gather for the huddle.

Hugs make little babies smile, and
puppies wag their tails,
Fuzzy kittens purr with joy and think you are swell!
No matter where you go the
language is always the same,
When a gracious hug is given no
one will ever complain.
So reach out with those loving
arms without any delay,
And give someone a great big
hug and make their day.

© January '2001

RAINDROPS

Raindrops, large and small –
They are tears of heaven, and
From God's eyes they fall.

© December 25, 2010

POET OR POETRY

The words I spin to gain thy love,
Which my darling shall I store?
Enduring love in my heart or words;
Should I decide with whom I adore?
To seek love in depths you do not know,
Words can't express true love for thee,
The anguish is to say it so elegantly,
Do you love the poet or poetry?

© September 22, 2001

FRECKLES

In her eyes you can see the glow,
And her figure shows through her dress,
But to paint her on the canvas of life
One must see the heart that beats in her breast.
Yes, her pretty face has freckles
That was sprinkled there by God's on hand,
But my heart skips a beat when I look in her eyes,
And I know I'm one lucky man!

If you were to touch the smoothness of her skin,
Your total self would be without strength,
For it's her smile, a beauty beyond mere words
That touches ones heart in depth and length.
Yes, her pretty face has freckles
But her soft voice is like beautiful music, too;
And when you hear her speak you're charmed,
Yes, she is mine, all mine, and not for you!

© December 22, 2004

A BOTTLE OF TIME

Man searches for answers over years of time
To understand the things that he can't see,
While the toil of the day passes on its way
With little thought of who or what he will be.

He starts his day with no thought of tomorrow
And in his arrogance he appears to be bold,
While often life is just a mere shadow of hope
And with his greed he seeks silver and gold.

But his Maker watches with a tearful eye
As man forever dashes to and fro,
While gathering the things that will soon fade
As the waters of his life move ever so slow.

God planned his days before he was born
Each day some good, while others not so fair,
Guided purposely over the years of time
It was placed before man with infinite care.

If man could see the beauty that's before him
And know that it is more valuable than gold
And accept the things that are beyond his reach,
Then he will find true peace within his soul.

Worry not about those things he cannot see,
And his sad heart would have no need to cry,
God in time will reveal His secrets to man
And he will no longer question the reasons why

Man's darkness will fade and there will be light
Given to a dark world made by God's own hand
This is more precious than all the silver and gold
For this is man's life in which He has planned.

© June 14, 2004

BETWEEN THE MIRROR

My life is but a moment
Between reality and me;
I cannot distinguish either
Nor my life's destiny.

I wonder about tomorrow,
With thoughts that coincide,
Did I forget about today?
While bound in foolish pride.

Thoughts falter in a silent mind,
And my eyes begin to cry
Between the mirror of imagination,
Are reflections of only why.

At times my heart is needful,
As words flow from my hands,
It matters not of today or tomorrow,
For only God knows my plans.

© May 3, 2008

CABIN BY THE MEADOW

The day will end as darkness falls,
And the sounds of night lets loose,
Within this stillness of the shadows
Where owls perch upon their roost.

Where light reflects from the water's edge,
And through life's stormy mist –
Are uncertain feelings within my soul?
That only time can surely resist.

Deep in my heart lies a subtle longing
For a place that I can come home to,
And where love lives at the end of the day,
Knowing that life is better because of you.

As I sit at the table and say my grace,
The smell in the room of a cooked meal,
And I know you have done this for me,
The troubles of my day I no longer feel.

From the front porch I watch the grass bend,
As the gentle winds blow with such ease,
And the times of sadness are gone forever,
Now songs of love are wonderful remedies.

My days shall not always be filled with comfort,
And troubles in life from which they begun,

Seem like raging storms beyond distant fields,
For now the silent rivers will slowly run.

Time will pass me quickly as clouds dissipate,
And the candles will burn upon the cake,
And time shall not wait for me to catch up,
Therefore I know that I must partake.

In your arms I feel safe as I hold you so tight,
The unspoken words and the tears I show,
Shall tell of a true love that was only for you,
As time drifts in the "cabin by the meadow."

© September 5, 2001

A PITTANCE OF TIME

Have you ever sat by a river's stream?
And listen to the sounds as you dream
Slowly aging like a vintage wine,-
It's only a moment in a pittance of time.
Brush strokes painted on a landscape
-God's gift for us to take.

I have-and to me its life's perfect scheme
Finding the time to do nothing but dream-
Of a friend-of a foe-or even an old flame-
Our dreams are here for us to claim,
As the water drifts slowly into a blue lake
-God's gift for us to take.

© November 20, 2006

DRAMA SO ODDLY

In the green meadow, clear and warm,
As summer breezes lay.
The petals I plucked,
And made my wishes,
And here I find,
The hidden imagines
Of a love
That is not to be found.

Upon the brink of time I stand
In a meadow
Of lost emotions,
The empty feelings
Among the flowers,
Where time moves
At its own pace.

The wind bends the silver grass,
Still wet with dew,
As the light dances the music
Of yesterday,
When I held her close,
And the world was ours.

In the green meadow, clear and warm,
Where webs are weaved,
And daisies fade in the sun,

Where sadness lingers
In a blue-shadowed sky,
Where time cannot erase
A love that is forevermore
Whispered upon the winds of time.

© May 25, 2003

WHY BLAME ME?

I want your lips when they're wet with wine,
And red with wild desire;
I want to look into your eyes when the love lights,
Lit with a passionate fire.
I want to feel your warm white flesh as it
Touches mine in a fond embrace,
I want my fingers in your hair and the strands enmesh
Your kisses against my face.

Do not give me the cold, meaningless kiss,
Of someone's bloodless love,
Not even the angel's white bless;
Nor the heart of a spotless dove.
But give me the love that so freely gives,
And laughs at the whole world outside,
With your warm and tender body lying in my arms,
It sets my heart and soul aflame.

My love, kiss me sweet with your warm wet mouth,
Still fragrant with ruby red wine,
And say with every emotion that you possess,
That your body and soul are mine.
Hold me close in your warm young arms,
While the misty stars shine above,
And we'll live the rest of our lives away,
In the joys of a pure living love . . .
Blame me for only loving you.

© '1999

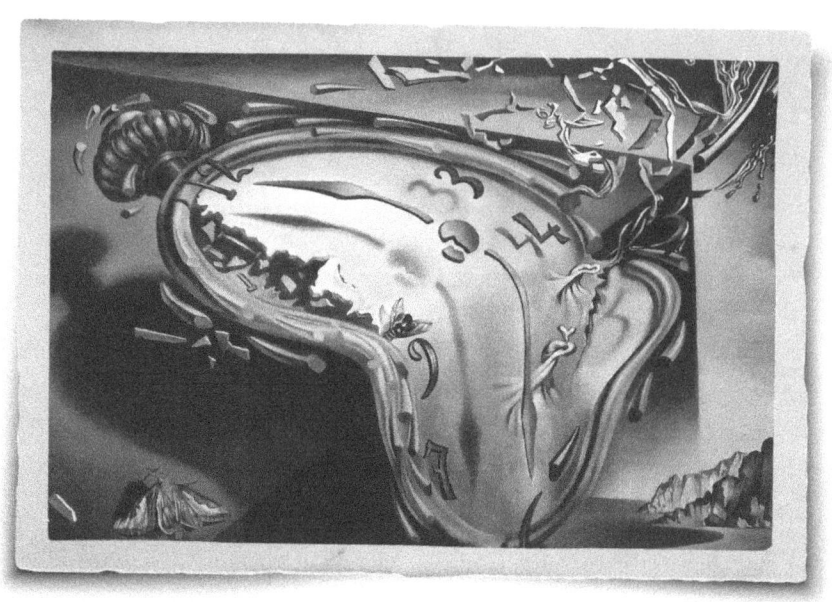

A MATTER OF TIME

God gives man his time only once,
And no man knows when that will end
For his days have been numbered,
And in the end death will always win.
This is the only life we will ever have.
So live, chariest, appreciate each day,
Take not one moment for granted
For life is short no matter what we say.

© August 4, 2006

CALM AS GLASS

This sadness that hides within me,
Was it lost in yesterday?
On the winds blowing by the sea,
Where spirits come out to play,
With gentle echoes of words,
Like whispers through the trees,
The sweet sounds of the birds,
And flowers were kissed by bees.
This sadness that hides within me,
Was thrown in the rivers of time,
And was carried out to the sea,
For these troubles shall not last,
And my heart will smile with joy,
In a soul as "calm as glass."

© October 6, 2001

ODE TO A ROSE

The earth brings forth your beauty so fair;
Your petals adorn the garments we wear,
To touch you is like majesty velvet light
That shines beneath the moon lit night.
The dew kisses you when you fall asleep,
As the soil wraps around your golden feet;
Your color is an array of beauty in the wind,
When hearts are saddened you become a friend.
Your fragrance intoxicates the air we breathe,
But you give hope to those that don't believe;
The mornings come to introduce your day,
And you stand tall and proud as if to say:
"Dear God! My beauty you have given man,
Brought forth from the thorns of your hand."

© January 6, 2003

FINGERS ENMESHED
IN YOUR HAIR

YOU can hear my broken heart cry
What is it saying to you?
Can you feel my pain!
I know you once loved me
I saw it in your eyes,
And when it comes to truth my heart cries
With this sadness of tears that fall quietly,
And I know it's my demise
To express this pain,
When I'm sitting all alone
Listening to the rain,
And I myself question if I'm going insane!
O this discontent, even the leaves and grass,
All lies dead upon the ground,
But soon this too shall pass –
My heart beats this longing sound…
And I know that you remember
My fingers enmeshed in your hair –
So my love, do you still care?
CAN you not hear my heart cry!
O this pain of loneliness…
And my sweet love only you know why.

© February 3, 2019

Fool me once,
shame on you.
Fool me twice,
shame on me.

FOOLS' LOVE

Upon memories I must draw,
And it's from a dream I saw;
You were reading a book as you sat by the pool;
Your beauty could make a man swear
And the wind was blowing your hair;
Then I ask myself do I love her or am I a fool?

Truth lies in the heart waiting to be told
One has to be ready for it to unfold;
It's like a cold drink of water to keep the lips cool;
The night still lingers on this sunny morn,
But to look upon her keeps my heart warm;
Then I ask myself does she love me or am I a fool?

© November 11, 2011

A FOG RISING

Can you hear…
The faint sounds of time,
Like little droplets of rain,
So quiet, so subtle, like a fog rising
At dawn …
The flowers kissed by the dew,
The birds waiting on the light,
And then…
Time unfolds the day,
So quiet, so subtle, as quietness calls
Your soul…
Then the crow calls from the field
To let us know:
That time waits on no one…

© January 7, 2024

53

CRAZY

THOSE crazy sounds in my head!
Words that rhyme – lost in my mind,

A happy spirit that my soul has fed –
Infinite thoughts most cannot find,
Hidden in the fog of gray matter,
And it feels like my head will shatter!
O where, O where is there solitude
It's like looking for Timbuktu!

Does it matter what has occurred
We're always looking beyond tomorrow,
But today will pass like a blur –
As the rivers of time continue to flow.
So I sit in the meadow plucking a daisy –
O the solitude! I just love being crazy!

© July 7, 2018

FACES OF EVIL

Monday's face was the same as we started our pace,
Tuesday's face is when terror rang with total disgrace,
Wednesday's face humiliated us with sorrow and woe,
Thursday's face gave us hope as we waited to know,
Friday's face showed despair as we wept with fear,
Saturday's face displayed our nation's eagle with a tear,
And our faces were humbly bowed before God on Sunday
To give us understanding for the evil that came our way.

© September 11, 2001

EMANCIPATED FROM CLAY

We were molded
Into a world of madness,
But who dictates our beliefs?
Is it acceptance we need?
Knowledge will set us free.
Wisdom has been penned,
But the world deceives us.
We know in our hearts the truth,
Yet we give in to others.
God is love…
His grace is sufficient
His hand is given with kindness
So take the path less traveled
Let your spirit be free
In time we all shall return
To the potters hands.

© October 26, 2002

A MOOT POINT

I saw the first light
as night fell—
the silent dawn
with sounds of blue
was a sadness within me,
as tears fell
my heart cried;
you will never know
how sadness feels,
when the fog rises
in this stillness.

Time I seek
Pauses not,
The wind sings a song,
And I know I'm alone.

O sweet music

god of the dawn,
I offer my confession—
do you hear, this sadness,
sweet God of reason,
take away my hurt;

these tears of dawn,
washes the hurt from
my eyes, red, blue,
with lack of sleep,
and whisky on my
breath or ginger ale;
no I can't tell
if this is a moot point,
my heart is hurting
from a night lost,
when love was all
I had to offer.

© September 8, 2007

Generation Z
different
devices
cool
demanding
future
change
housing
confident
video
community
lifestyle
native
gadgets
digital
rapid
smart
prospects
restless
business
social
ambitious
priorities
online
teenagers
innovation
underemployed
games
impulsive
youth
innovative
technology
connected
healthy
leader
web
education
inspiration
rules
economy
computer
mobility
blog

GENERATION 'Z'

I wonder why people can't do anything
They just sit around and complain!

The rhetoric is a damaging sound –
If you listen too much it gets you down.

You like a good debate just as much as I,
But this generation makes me sigh.

The youth, they are too damn young,
Listen to what rolls off their tongue.

They need to go to work – well pitch a fit,
But to get a head it takes a lot of grit!

I know the truth makes you squirm –
But the lessons of life you need to learn.

"He who works the best will find rest,"
And work it will take to pass life's test.

© February 1, 2023

HERE ON EARTH

When the apple is ripe it will drop,
The seasons will come and go,
And there are things we'll never know:
But things go on without a stop –
Look at the mountains standing tall
The streams – we can't count them all!

So we have to live life and do our best,
All things both great and small –
There is no way we can hate it all,
But though I have to say life was a test:
It's is just a journey from our birth
A chance we were given here on earth!

So please stop and look all around …
As the apples lie quietly upon the ground.

© January 30, 2024

SOUND OF SILENCE

The world is too noise for us; sonic blooms,
Planes and trains, with all their mighty powers:
Little is left in life that we can call ours;
How have we come to this, where noise looms?
The silence has lost meaning beneath the moon;
The traffic that rushes on and on for hours,
Never enough time to stop and smell the flowers;
Tell me, for what, have we given up life's sweet tune;
When will it stop?—Dear God! Noise want let us be
In a time when we need to look inward;
So silence, please calm our minds and let us see,
A simple time that doesn't reflect outward;
Like when the wind kisses the leaves of a tree;
Oh the sound of silence that's seldom heard.

© August 19, 2004

TEARDROPS OF AUTUMN

A lonely heart can't sleep at night
While the night sounds are calling,
Calling from the secret places of time,
And here the heart lies crying…

Teardrops of autumn needs to weep,
And the heartaches inside can't sleep,

O how I feel like there is no tomorrow,
And this darkness is filled with sorrow,

How can this heart bear such sadness?
How, memories rush in from yesterday
When love was good – love at its best,
But now the chill of autumn has its way!

Doubt and fear now whispers in my ears,
And how am I to tell them apart…
The wind howls as if it needs to cry –
While this despair grips my broken heart.

Teardrops of autumn hear my sad chant
For it seems this night I need to rant!

Autumn has come in the sadness of life,
And now I have to face all of this strife,

With sad thoughts the devil has his way,
But through my sadness I need to say:

Tomorrow the sun will surely be shining,
And life, it's just a mountain I'm climbing.

© September 8, 2015

THE WRETCHED MAN AM I

Each day as I make my way
My inner self is filled with doubt
Feels so deep that it won't come out
Hidden in the darkness of my soul,
But I go on day after day,

Consumed in this quietness,
Going here and going there,
Hoping yet this day will soon pass
When I will no longer think of you,
And time shall wither like the grass.

In the depths of my soul,
In a place where sadness stirs,
Thoughts of nowhere to go,
My eyes reflect only blurs,
For time is now dim where I lie,
And dark clouds hang in the sky.

If you knew me you would run away,
The sadness inside a soul bound,
With life's endless negative sound,
Hidden from the world's view;
In darkness where shadows stirs
In the quietness of the mires,
No one dares to look under my mask
Is this truth to much for you?

If you would come sit for a day,
I would share these secrets with you,
I promise I will not run away
Though this is hard for me to do
The truth will set me free,

And should you want to stay,
My soul would make a joyous sound,
This heart would surely turn around,
And your acceptance is with gratitude!
In this place where nothing stirs
Like the fog lifting upon the mires.

In this life I only seek to find
That I'd no longer think as they;
I would take a different view,
And have better thoughts in mind
If only I had you,
And this wretched man am I…
Would find reasons to live another day.

© August 25, 2003

RED OCTOBER

Beware! It is Red October,
Be vigilant, and be sober!
The tide is about to change,
The stars will be rearranged –
Things of yesterday are dead
This is going to spin your head!
No longer will we be in despair
At work, or play, or in prayer –
You will not need to guess
About the gnawing emptiness!
Beware! It's an October tide,
Your hearts will burst with pride!
And to God we humbly pray…
"Red October" you saved the day.

© October 1, 2018

JUST OLD LETTERS

Sometimes it's hard to express
The emotions that is so deep,
I have no flags to wave here
There're only thoughts I keep.

Just old boxes stacked in a corner
It's funny how time slips away –
But I guess it's time to make a path,
So I brushed the dust away…

Hidden beneath some old books
Were letters from years gone by?
The pages were bent and brown –
And as I read them I begin to cry...

The emotions that is so deep,
O how I've tried to put them away!
But like a tide they come rushing in –
A love so deep there is a price to pay!

Each word is followed by a tear,
And I seem to hear her voice...
And in my soul there is this longing,
And it bids my heart to rejoice...

No! They are not just old letters,
And not mere words upon a page –
But it's a part of something I lost,
And they calm a spirit that's in rage!

The emotions that is so deep,
So I return them to their sacred place –
My hands tremble, and my heart cries,
"Love is forever"– this I have to face!

© July 10, 2000

TEMPUS FUGIT

The roses, they smell like honey,
The autumn day drifts slowly,
The heart of men only seeks money
Though his riches are never enough,
The daises in the field will soon wilt,
The reality of time fades with each day,
But how I know, the sorrows I've built,
And the times I could not find my way.

The world turns ever so quickly,
But the shadows still linger on the hill –
The sounds of her voice I hear so clearly,
But time has a way of stealing my will.
The clouds come rushing in from above,
Brings the coldness of an October rain,
But it is her heart that I still love,
And this loneliness I can never contain.

© April 23, 2004

STARY-STARY NIGHT

Into the darkness of night!
  Like a sea's endless deeps,
Beyond the hidden light!
  She weeps!
My lover weeps!
  And weeps!

Moon drifts in the evening night!
Even as she sleeps,
Beneath the shadows of light!
She weeps!
My lover weeps!
And weeps!

Sadness shows up at night!
Where hurt and pain creeps,
Where only stars give out light!
She weeps!
My lover weeps!
And weeps!

She dreams of love at night!
She prays for her soul He keeps!
Wishing to see tomorrow's light
She weeps!
My lover weeps!
For a love she seeks!

© February 27, 2012

GREETINGS
FROM HELL

Remember her on that forgotten day,
Mania Halef, just a small child of two;
The sights of horror her eyes did view,
Not a life she'd have, nor a time of play.
Remember her if some should try to say:
"It didn't happen", stand up with us few,
And tell the world that this story is true –
It's not too late for man to kneel and pray,
And ask forgiveness for that horrible day;
The hatred in men that could never grieve
A life of a child, and hurts it would leave
Greetings from hell were thoughts she had,
How can we forget the horrors she knew?
Her walk to Babi Yar should leave us sad.

© January 7, 2007

AT LEAST I TRIED

The adversity I've had to endure
It was worse than being dragged
Through the sewer!
But all in all I have stood tall,
And with God's help I endured it all!
There are winners, and they're losers
Caviar and connoisseurs…
Some say we are just dreamers
Seeking riches and following schemers,
But everything in life is a roll of the dice,
And I forgive you for not being nice!
What is life, if you don't take a chance?
You know, it always takes two to dance!
You see life is just a game . . .
And if I lose it's only me I have to blame!
But this I can say, at least I tried –
And over losing I've never cried!

© January 25, 2024

PROMISES OF GOD

There were flowers placed by her grave,
And beautiful words the man had to say –
A lady was singing Amazing Grace…
And my tears I could not wipe away!
The autumn sun was bright and warm,
And there was a smell of a field nearby –
Memories were rushing through my mind,
And our girls beside me begin to cry!
From the woods a crow gives out a call –
I noticed a bee on the spray of flowers,
And it was a day that I will never forget!
The ceremony was short, and not hours,
(I held you – you took your last breath)
But God promises us life even after death.

© October 23, 2020

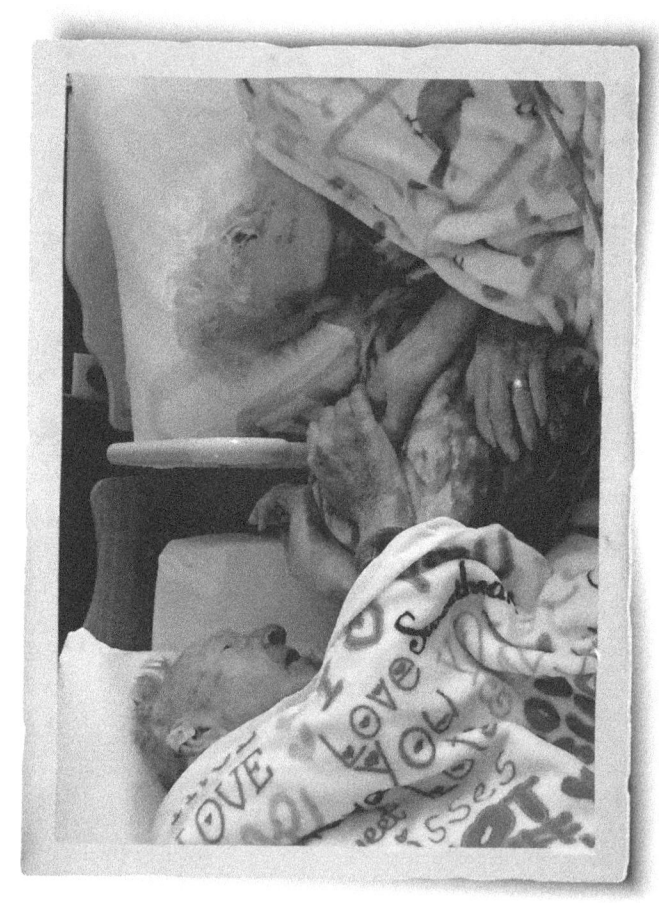

AMERICA'S PRAYER

O America! Kneel down and pray,
And to a forgiving God we need to say:
O Lord, bless this land, O mighty God!
Give back the things the enemy robbed.
Let us turn our eyes upon the cross,
Let us all pray for those that are lost –
Dear Lord let us return back to You
Respect for others and our President too!
Let us return to the values of yesterday…
Give us another chance O Lord, we pray!
Let the bells of freedom ring with peace,
Stop all of the hatred – let it all cease!
Guide President Trump whom we adore,
Help him with the burdens he must bore!

© July 27, 2017

BONDAGE NO MORE!

O how I have heard the cries of My children,
And Egypt, you will set my people free!
My prophecy shall be fulfilled as it is written:
"Pharaoh will send the children of Israel
Out of his land and the Egyptians will give
Israel all their wealth to get rid of them."
So shall it be in latter days before God's return,
The meek, for they shall inherit the earth;
Wealth will increasingly find and overtake us,
For the purpose is to establish God's covenant.
Honour the Lord with thy substance, and with
The first fruits of all thine increase. Thou hast
Caused men to ride over our heads, we went
Through fire and through water, but thou
Broughtest us out into a wealthy place. Behold,
God has allowed the wicked to accumulate all
Kinds of treasures for His use in the last days.
Be patient therefore, brethren, unto the coming
Of the Lord, the husbandman waiteth for the
Precious fruit of the earth, until he receive the
Early and latter rain, outpouring of God's
Spirit is for the harvest of souls into the body
Of Christ and of God. Be ye also patient, establish
Your hearts, for the coming of the Lord draweth
Nigh to restore the wealth into the hands of
God's people. Amen!

© April 27, 2013

ONLY GOD IS WISE

To the stars I look, but they're not awake!
Its wisdom I need and I've looked in others eyes –
In time it will come, but I will have to wait,
"But the truth is," it's only God that is wise.

O the heart breaks of life I have seen…
And the loneliness that seems to come at night –
But to the stars I still look, and I still dream…
For out of the darkness there is always light!

Endless hours spent – others I tried to please!
Unclean words can't be scraped from the tongue,
And maybe I have spoken the worst of these –
Is it the nature of men – we are a bit high strung.

Its wisdom I need and I've looked in others eyes –
"But the truth is," it's only God that is wise.

© February 20, 2020

BLAST OF THE SHOFAR

I dreamt I heard a blast over the land,
A sound of a Shofar from God's own hand,
And it said to me with such clarity –
"Take heed my child this message from Me."
For I have always been with you at every turn-
And I've taught you the things you needed to learn.
I have given you the songs that angels have known,
And I have promised I'd never leave you alone;
The clouds will open, and My blessings shall flow
These are the promises that you were told.
So be a good steward and give a portion back to Me,
And the blessings of a long life you will see;
This is a gift of love and not one from men,
It is of the Father's doings, and so then
I will sit in heaven knowing that I did My part,
This blessing to you My child is from My heart.

© October 11, 2009

VIOLINS OF MY SOUL

In the stillness of my soul
The sad sounds of the violin:
Ask "where has passion gone?"
How can I endure this loneliness?
When the night becomes still.

I'm sure when a hundred years pass
Others will ask this very question:
"How can one live without passion?"
But we only see what is before us
With little thought of a true love;

One that reaches to the pit of existence
Where passion cries inside the heart!

In the stillness of time
The violin cries with sadness,
And tears stream from my eyes;
It's here in this silence…
Where I can hear my heart beat,
And it aches for the love it needs.

What is my purpose here if not to love?
To taste the fruits of your passion,
To lie upon the satin sheets with you,
And to absorb the sweetness of life…
And listen to the violins of my soul.

© March 12, 2011